LOOKING INSIDE

MACHINES AND CONSTRUCTIONS

STATUE OF LIBERTY

Liberty Enlightening the World stands on Liberty Island in New York Harbor. The statue was designed by the French sculptor Frédéric-Auguste Bartholdi and was completed in 1886. She is 151 feet high and stands on a 154-foot pedestal. Visitors are allowed to climb the 354 spiraling steps to her crown.

Liberty is made of three hundred thick copper sheets that were shaped by hammering them into molds. The copper sheets are supported on a framework of steel beams and four columns. The framework was designed by Alexandre-Gustave Eiffel, the designer of the Eiffel Tower. The pedestal is made of concrete reinforced with steel and is covered with blocks of granite. In 1986, Liberty was restored and given a new, gold-covered torch.

LOOKING INSIDE
MACHINES AND CONSTRUCTIONS

WRITTEN BY
PAUL FLEISHER & PATRICIA A. KEELER

ILLUSTRATED BY PATRICIA A. KEELER

ATHENEUM 1991 NEW YORK

Collier Macmillan Canada
TORONTO

Maxwell Macmillan International Publishing Group
NEW YORK OXFORD SINGAPORE SYDNEY

To Bette Russell Keeler, who taught me how to match plaids
—*P.A.K.*

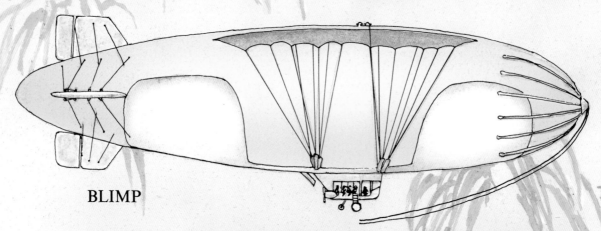

BLIMP

A blimp is a huge bag, or "envelope," of rubber-coated fabric, filled with light helium gas. The Goodyear blimp is 192 feet long, weighs only 9,500 pounds, and holds over 200,000 cubic feet of gas. It can travel 50 miles per hour and carries up to six passengers.

Inside the envelope are two smaller bags filled with air. These "ballonets" let the pilot raise or lower the blimp's nose or tail and adjust for changes in air pressure. The pilot steers by moving the elevators and rudders on the ship's tail. The pilot and passengers ride in a gondola at the bottom of the blimp. The gondola hangs from cables attached to the top of the envelope.

ACKNOWLEDGMENTS. Thanks to the following people and organizations for their help in researching this book: C&P Telephone, Clock Shop of Richmond, Ernie Dean, Dan Fleisher, Goodyear Tire and Rubber, Dr. Phillip Ianna, King's Dominion, Little Yogurt Shop, National Air and Space Museum, National Aquarium in Baltimore, Gary Senechal, Perey Turnstiles, Richmond Department of Street Cleaning, Richmond Piano, Statue of Liberty National Monument, United Technologies Hamilton Standard, Dion Wheeler, and especially Francis McCall.

Atheneum
Macmillan Publishing Company
866 Third Avenue
New York, New York 10022

Collier Macmillan Canada, Inc.
1200 Eglinton Avenue East
Suite 200
Don Mills, Ontario M3C 3N1

Printed in Hong Kong

10 9 8 7 6 5 4 3 2 1

Library of Congress Cataloging-in-Publication Data

Fleisher, Paul.
    Looking inside: machines and constructions / written by Paul Fleisher and Patricia A. Keeler; illustrated by Patricia A. Keeler. — 1st ed.
        p.   cm.
    Summary: Describes the interior of such objects as a piano, telephone, clock, toilet, and camera, and explains how these devices work.
    ISBN 0-689-31483-3
    1. Technology—Juvenile literature. 2. Machinery—Juvenile literature. [1. Technology. 2. Machinery.] I. Keeler, Patricia A., ill. II. Title.
T48.F54 1991   90–743
600—dc20   CIP
                                                    AC

CONTENTS

PIANO

Each key on the piano is a lever, which lifts up a complex set of connected wooden parts. As they move, these pieces make a padded wooden hammer hit a metal piano string. When the hammer strikes it, this tight wire vibrates to make a sound of just the right pitch. When the pianist takes her finger off the key, a pad touches the string, stopping the sound.

The piano strings stretch across a wedge-shaped wooden bridge, which also vibrates when the string is struck. The bridge transfers the vibrations to a thin sounding board made of spruce. The entire board vibrates, making the sound much louder.

The pedals of a piano move another set of levers up and down. One pedal brings the hammers closer to the strings, so the piano plays more softly. Another allows the strings to keep vibrating after the pianist has lifted her fingers from the keys.

STEAM IRON

The metal base of a steam iron is hollow.
Water from a small tank in the top of the iron
trickles down into a chamber in the center of the
base. In the chamber is a heating element, like
the burner on an electric stove. When the iron is
turned on, the element heats the surrounding
metal and turns the water to steam.

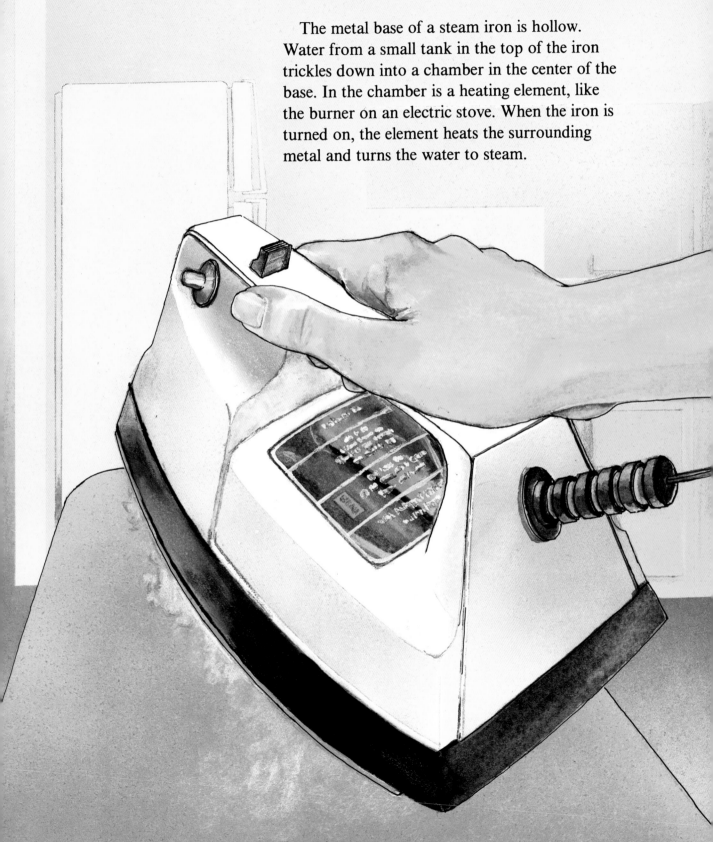

The steam flows through the many passageways in the metal and out the small holes in the bottom of the iron. Steam helps take the wrinkles out of clothes.

The iron's control knob adjusts a metal strip. Because the strip is made of two different metals, it bends as it gets cooler or hotter. Depending on which way it bends, it makes or breaks electrical contact with another wire strip. This special switch, called a thermostat, turns the heating element on and off, keeping the iron at the right temperature.

WALL

Most buildings have hollow double walls. Outer walls are made of wood, brick, stone, aluminum, or vinyl. Inner walls are usually made of wallboard, a sandwich of plasterlike gypsum between pieces of cardboard.

Builders use the space between the walls for important "services." Electrical wires are hidden in the walls. So are water pipes for sinks, toilets, and other plumbing fixtures. Larger waste pipes take wastewater out of the buildings to the sewers.

The walls of modern buildings are insulated with plastic foam or fiberglass. Insulation helps keep the buildings warm in winter and cool in summer.

TELEPHONE

Dialing a telephone sends electrical signals to the phone company offices. The signals tell a computer where to connect the call. The telephone mouthpiece turns the sound vibrations of each speaker's voice into electrical signals that travel through wires or by radio.

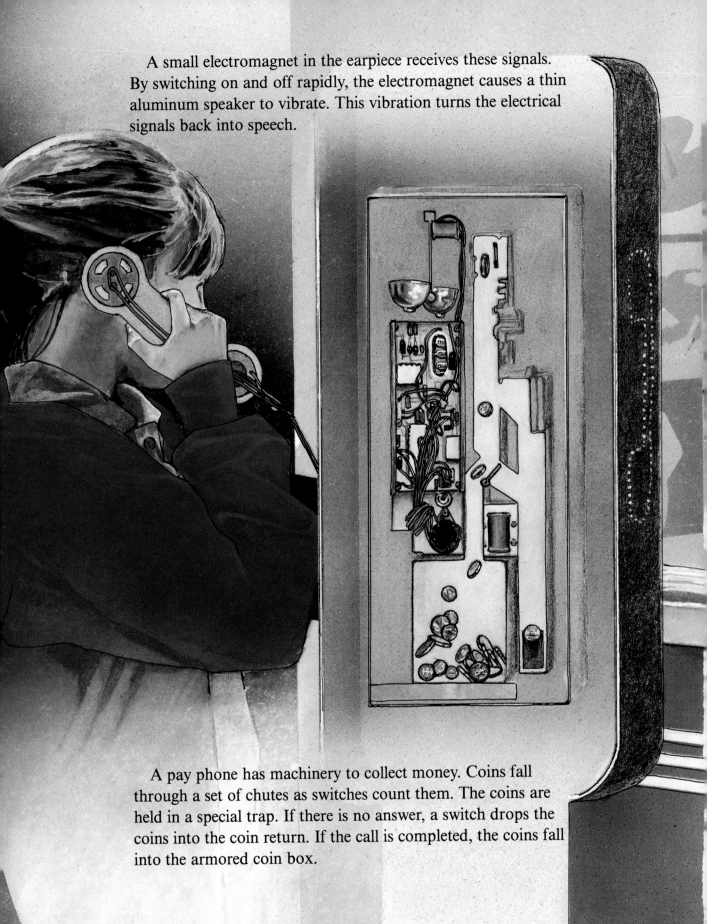

A small electromagnet in the earpiece receives these signals. By switching on and off rapidly, the electromagnet causes a thin aluminum speaker to vibrate. This vibration turns the electrical signals back into speech.

A pay phone has machinery to collect money. Coins fall through a set of chutes as switches count them. The coins are held in a special trap. If there is no answer, a switch drops the coins into the coin return. If the call is completed, the coins fall into the armored coin box.

TURNSTILE

A turnstile controls the movement of people through an entrance or exit. The turnstile's arms are attached to a toothed ratchet wheel inside the machine. As people push past, they turn the wheel. A small metal piece called a pawl catches each notch between the teeth. The pawl prevents the turnstile from turning back in the other direction.

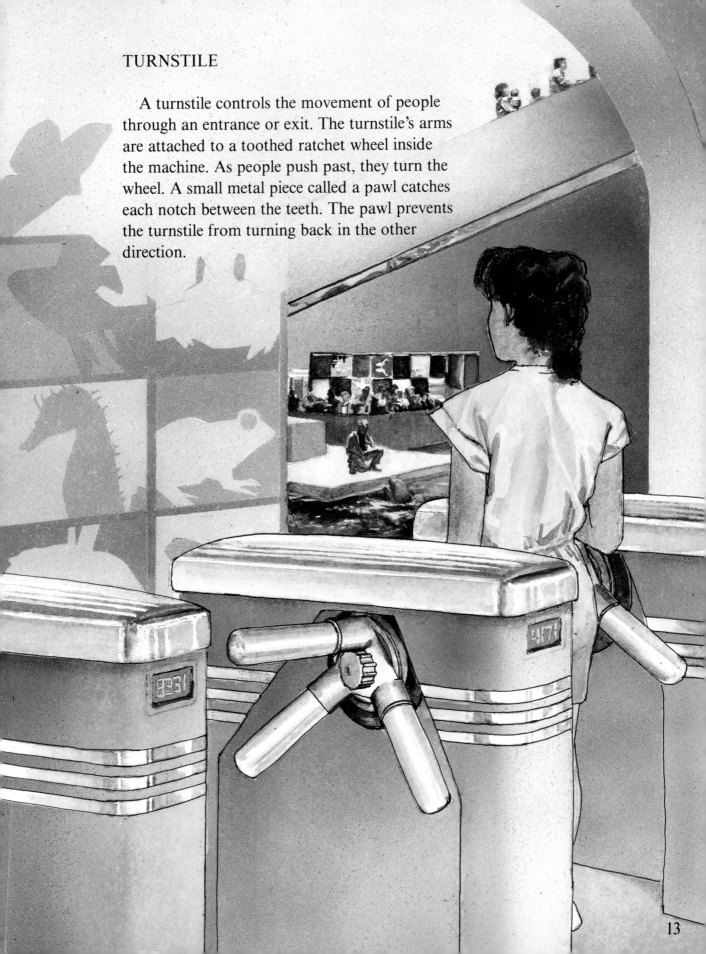

Three round, rolling pegs—called studs—are attached to the wheel and turn with it. Strong springs hold two curved, metal "shoes" against the studs. The shoes force the turnstile to spin smoothly and bring it to a stop at just the right place.

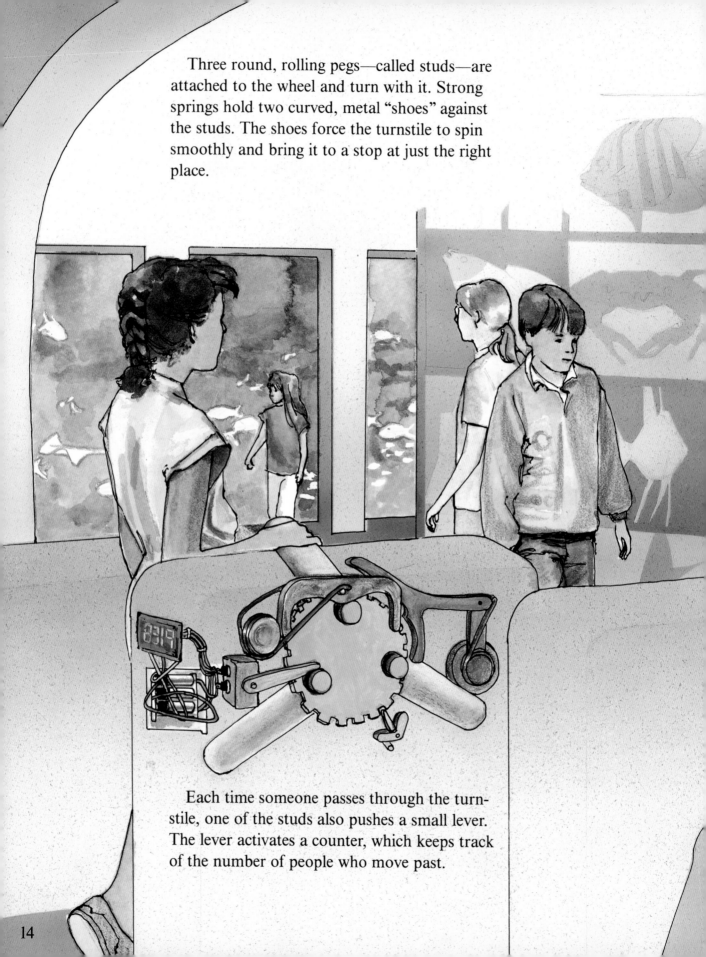

Each time someone passes through the turnstile, one of the studs also pushes a small lever. The lever activates a counter, which keeps track of the number of people who move past.

CLOCK

The mechanical clock was invented in the 1600s. Clocks have changed very little in the four hundred years since.

As it slowly unwinds, the steel mainspring provides power to turn the gears. When the mainspring winds down, turning a key at the back of the clock tightens it again.

The balance wheel acts as the clock's timing device. It always spins back and forth at exactly the same speed. The pallet fork pushes the balance wheel in one direction. Then the delicate spiral hairspring spins it back the other way. The balance wheel rocks the crescent-shaped pallet back and forth as it spins. As it rocks, the pallet catches and releases each notch of the escape wheel. This controls how quickly the gears move and makes the familiar ticking sound. The gears are just the right size to keep accurate time as they move the clock's hands.

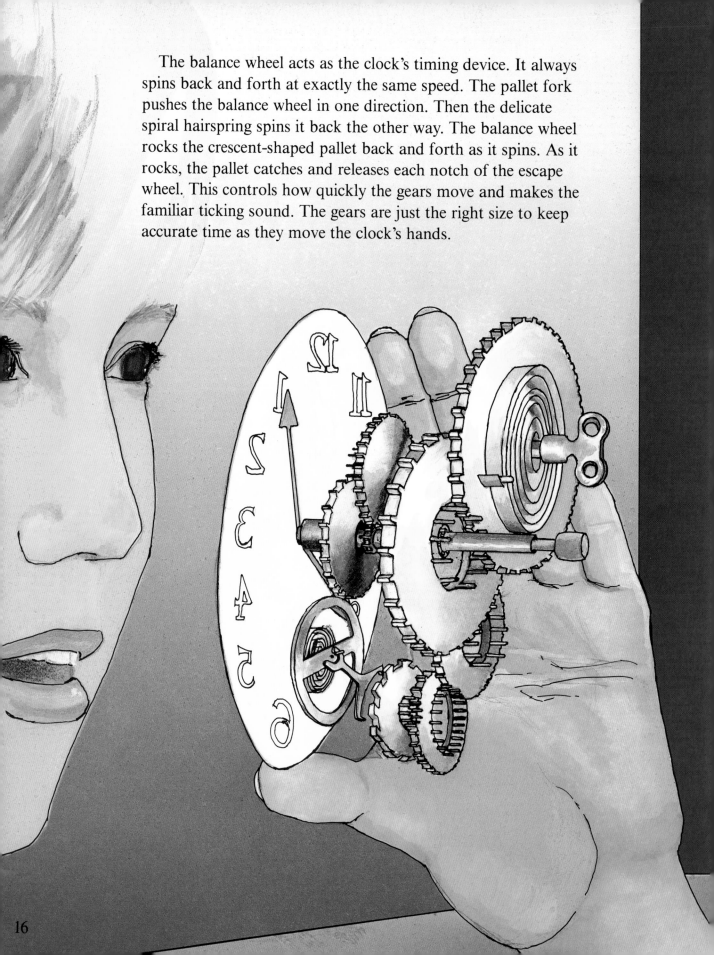

AQUARIUM

The puffins at the National Aquarium in Baltimore come from arctic seas. Air conditioners cool their room to 45 degrees Fahrenheit.

The "rocks" in the tank are made of fiberglass and a type of cement. The glass in front of the tank has two separate half-inch layers, to insulate the tank and help keep it cool.

The puffins' lights are regulated by a timer, so the birds seem to experience changing seasons even though they are indoors. The lights brighten and dim slowly each day, to imitate normal sunrise and sunset.

The water in the tank is pumped through screens that filter out feathers. Then, a sand-and-gravel filter removes smaller particles. Finally, the water goes through a cooling unit, where its temperature is also lowered to 45 degrees before it is pumped back into the tank. Once a week, everything is scrubbed and disinfected, and the birds get a complete change of water.

ESCALATOR

An escalator, or moving stairway, is a chain of stair steps. It rolls endlessly around a set of rollers, much like a bicycle chain. A powerful electric motor keeps the stairway moving.

Handrails moving at the same speed as the steps help people keep their balance. At the end of the escalator, the steps disappear under a flat plate, which helps people step off the stairway safely and easily.

Escalators were invented in the 1890s. They became popular in large stores in the 1920s and 1930s. Because they move constantly, escalators can transport many more people between floors than elevators can.

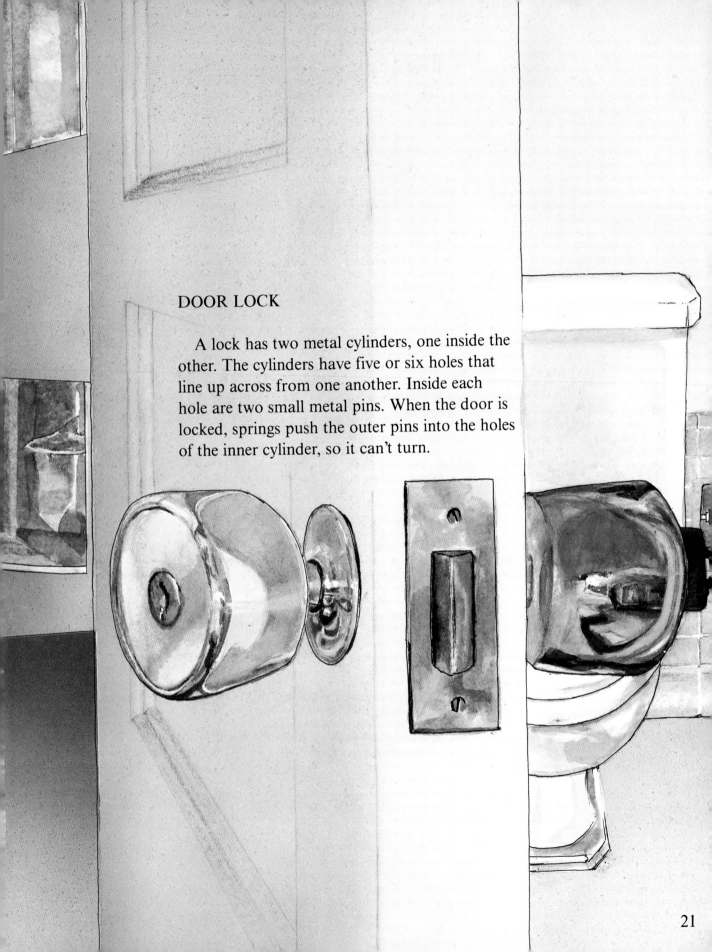

DOOR LOCK

A lock has two metal cylinders, one inside the other. The cylinders have five or six holes that line up across from one another. Inside each hole are two small metal pins. When the door is locked, springs push the outer pins into the holes of the inner cylinder, so it can't turn.

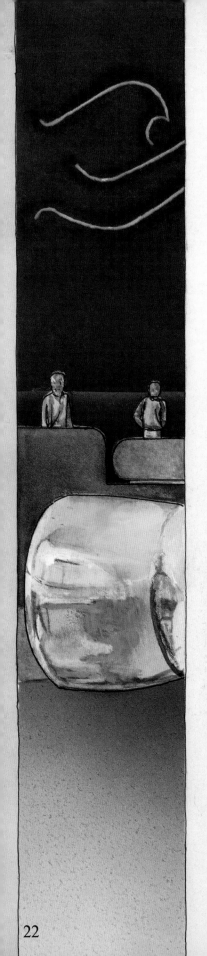

The key lifts the pins of the inner cylinder to just the right height. The inner pins push the outer pins back into the outer cylinder. That allows the key to turn the inner cylinder.

When the cylinder turns, a part of the latching machinery is moved out of the way. This allows the door handle to turn. The handle lifts a lever, which pulls back the door latch so the door can be opened.

TOILET

A toilet is made of baked clay, with a glassy finish that helps keep it clean. The toilet tank holds about three gallons of water. When the handle is pushed, it opens the flush valve in the bottom of the tank. The water from the tank pours into the toilet bowl, swirling and washing down the sides.

The rising water in the bowl fills the curved pathway to the waste pipe at the back of the toilet. Gravity and the pressure of the water then force the contents of the bowl down the waste pipe.

When the tank is empty, the flush valve closes. Another valve, called a ball cock, opens to let water in to refill the tank. A float attached to that valve rises with the rising water. When the float rises to the correct level, the ball cock closes so no more water can enter. The tank has a small overflow tube, which prevents the water level from getting too high.

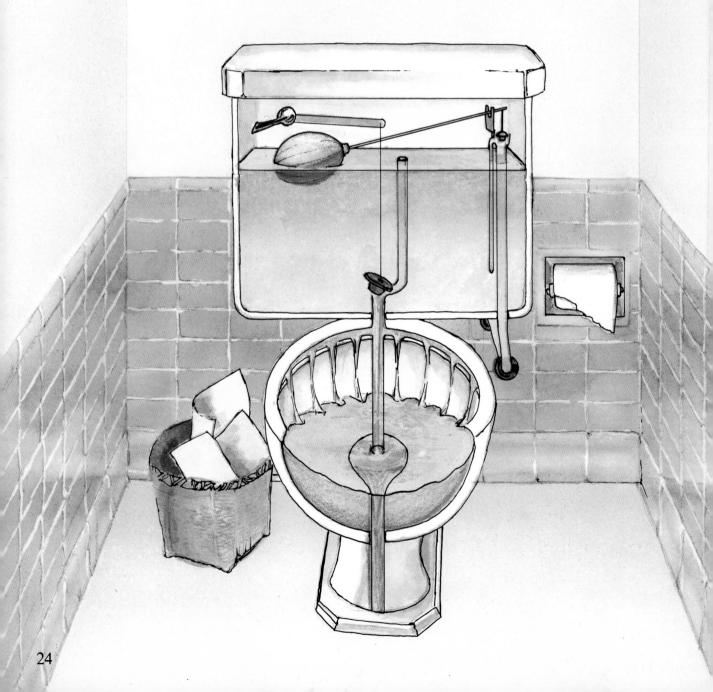

STREET SWEEPER

A street sweeper has
round, stiff, steel brushes on
each side. These brushes
sweep all the trash toward
the center of the machine.
The brushes are powerful
enough to pick up bricks!

At the back of the machine is a long, round brush with plastic bristles. It pushes the trash up onto a slanted metal slide. Thick rubber squeegees carry the trash up the slide and into a big collecting bin.

When the bin is full, powerful hydraulic arms lift it up and dump the trash into a waiting truck.

The street sweeper carries about three hundred gallons of water in a tank. Nozzles underneath the sweeper spray the street ahead of the brushes, so dust doesn't fly into the air as the brushes whirl by.

CAMERA

A camera collects light through its lens. The lens focuses the light on film to make the picture. The photographer looks at a reflection of the scene through the viewfinder. She adjusts the focus of the lens by turning one of its rings. The photographer turns another ring to adjust the iris, or opening, of the lens. This allows just the right amount of light into the camera.

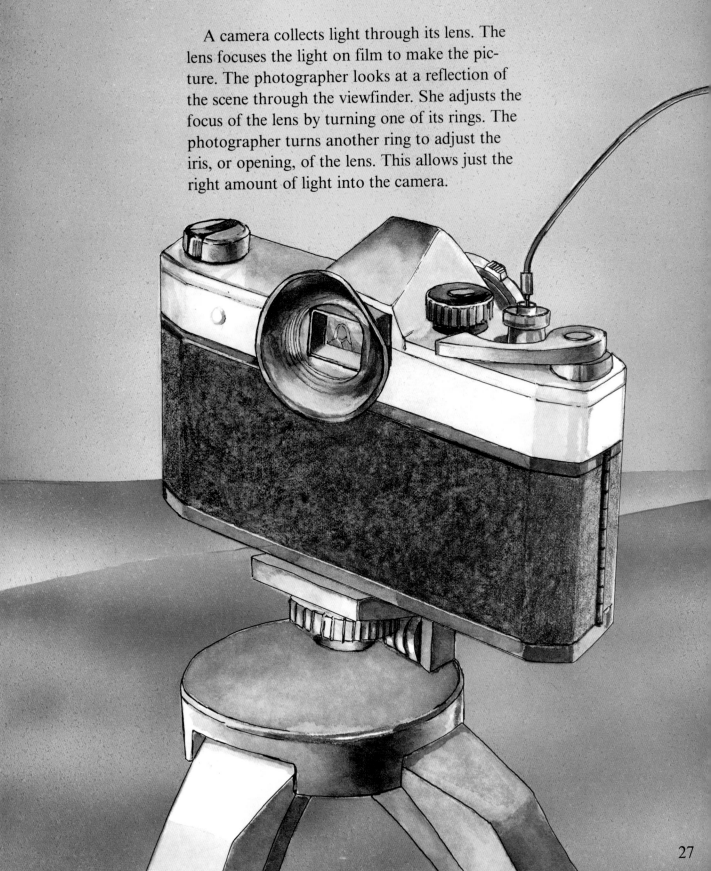

When the photographer pushes the shutter button, the viewfinder's mirror is lifted out of the way. Then the shutter opens for a fraction of a second. Light comes into the camera and shines on the film. This causes a chemical reaction on the film, which creates a picture.

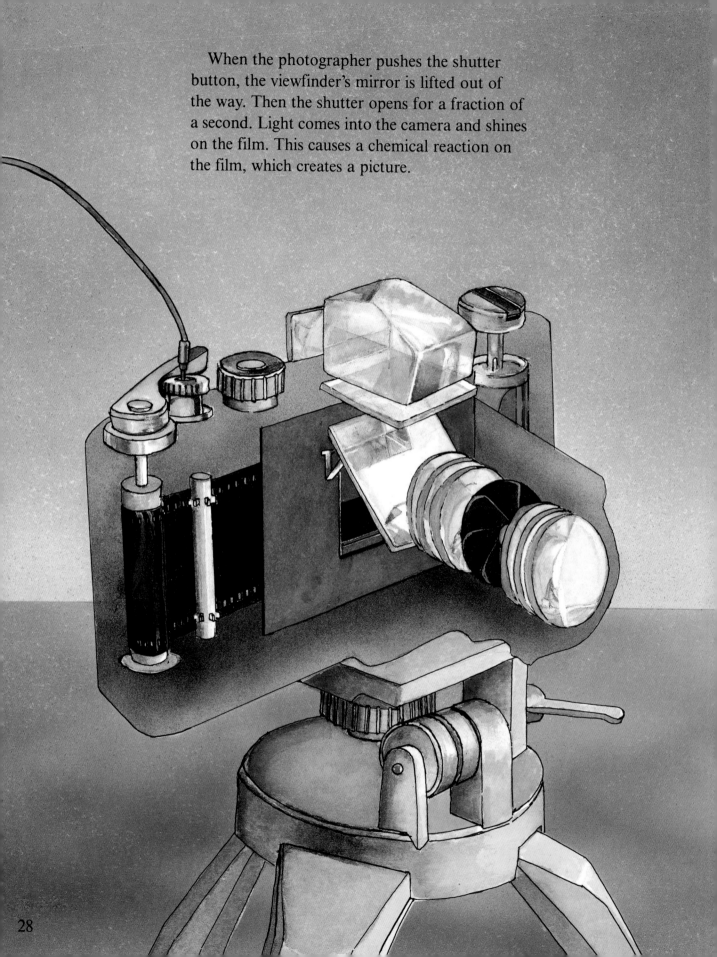

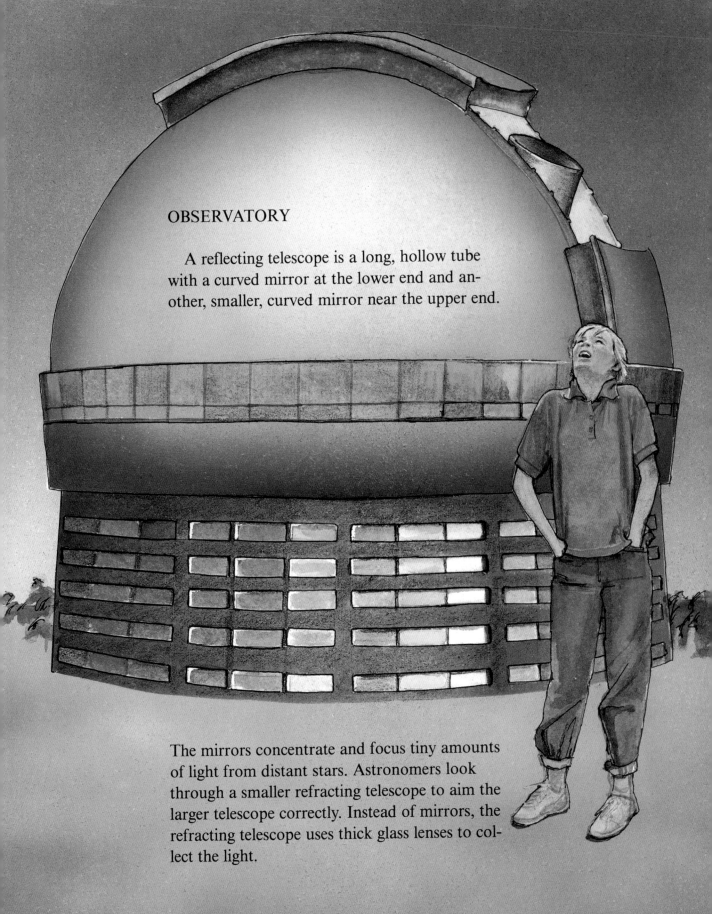

OBSERVATORY

A reflecting telescope is a long, hollow tube with a curved mirror at the lower end and another, smaller, curved mirror near the upper end.

The mirrors concentrate and focus tiny amounts of light from distant stars. Astronomers look through a smaller refracting telescope to aim the larger telescope correctly. Instead of mirrors, the refracting telescope uses thick glass lenses to collect the light.

Starlight enters the upper end of the tube. The large mirror at the lower end reflects the light back to the smaller mirror. That mirror reflects the light back to the lower end. Each reflection concentrates the dim starlight into a smaller, brighter image. At the lower end, a light-sensitive computer chip records the light it "sees" and displays the information on a video screen.

SPACE SUIT

The arms and legs of the space suit are made of many layers of flexible cloth and plastic. Cooling water is pumped through thousands of thin tubes in the innermost layer of the suit. The water carries away extra body heat as the astronaut works. The outer layers hold in the pressurized oxygen, insulate against the extreme temperatures of space, and protect the suit, and astronaut, against damage.

The U.S. Extravehicular Mobility Unit (EMU) weighs 250 pounds. It has everything an astronaut needs to stay alive for six hours—oxygen, cooling water, and batteries to run lights, fans, pumps, radios to communicate with the space shuttle, and a tiny computer.

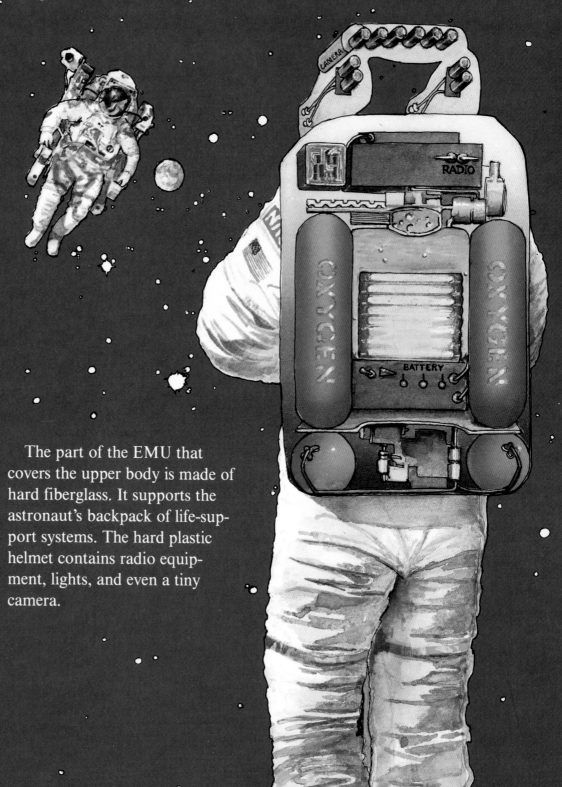

The part of the EMU that covers the upper body is made of hard fiberglass. It supports the astronaut's backpack of life-support systems. The hard plastic helmet contains radio equipment, lights, and even a tiny camera.